Fleeting Glimpses

of

The Silly, Sentimental and Sublime

Michael Seagriff

Fleeting Glimpses

of

The Silly, Sentimental and Sublime

Interior photographs © Michael Seagriff

ISBN - 13: 978-0692210765
ISBN - 10: 0692210768

Printed in the United States of America

Michael Seagriff
Canastota, New York

<u>Dedication</u>

To my wife Lonnie -for her unlimited
love, support and encouragement.

Table of Contents

(Sit down)

INTRODUCTION

St. Thomas Aquinas, the greatest of all Catholic theologians, stopped writing after a mystical vision convinced him that all he had put down on paper was of little value, like so much "straw in the wind".

I am no Aquinas and this little work is not worthy to be used as a bookmark in his *Summa Theologiae*. Why then would a simple man like me compile such a disparate assortment of personal memories and reflections?

Because I believe there is still a market for "straw"! After all, it has been used for centuries to protect emerging vegetative growth from the destructive force of the sun's rays and as nourishment and bedding. Straw can at least forestall hunger and cold for a time until more substantive food and shelter arrive.

It is my hope then that something you read here might bring you laughter at a time you feel forlorn, comfort when you are overburdened with the challenges of daily living, tears of joy when certain words you read or images they generate resurrect thoughts of those you loved and lost, greater appreciation for the gift of life, zeal for the salvation of your soul, and an increased desire to give to God and those He created what He and they deserve.

Remember this is just "straw". Don't linger here. Go to the Source.

(Relax)

Smooth As Silk

There was a time in my life when I loved Friday nights – the night I would lace up those barely used sneakers, take two aspirin, drive to the Durhamville elementary school and relive past days of glory on the hardwood with eleven other middled age, overweight and out of shape basketball wannabes. Oh, the joy and pain each Friday brought - performing feats on the court unseen by anyone else save my trusted basketball buddies. That was all about to change.

"Dad," my daughter Tammy screamed as I limped in through the side door following a particularly grueling evening of competition. "The Lady Raiders are having a fundraiser. The Buffalo Bills are coming to play a game against our teachers and parents, and you're on the team!"

My two daughters and son were talented basketball players who had given their parents and fans years of enjoyment. Tammy had been a star on her varsity team since the eighth grade. "It is all in the genes," I mused. Now the tables would be reversed. My children would be sitting in the stands and I would be working my magic on the court. Now all their fans would know the source of their incredible skills.

Visions of grandeur immediately floated through my deluded mind. I could just picture the adoring throng of fans chanting my name, demanding the coach unleash my talent upon the assembled but unsuspecting professional athletes who would soon regret having accepted this challenge. Finally, someone other than my buddies will see what astonishing illusions I could work. Little did I know then, how much they would actually see.

It wasn't very long before our team was down 18 points. There was still five minutes left in the first quarter. "Put me in coach," I pleaded, voicing what I suspected was the unspoken desire of the fans that had filled the brown rickety bleacher seats to overflowing. "You and Pete (the only other parent on this team) might as well go in," mumbled a less than enthusiastic player-coach. "Let someone else embarrass themselves."

1

The fact that I was about to play against kicker Scott Norwood, wide receiver Steve Tasker, linebacker Shane Conlan, and backup quarterbacks, Frank Reich and Stan Gelbaugh, caused me no concern. I looked at Pete. He glared back into my eyes. We were ready.

I heard my wife and kids screaming out my name. I even heard a few of my enthusiastic clients doing likewise. Was that a poster with my name that I saw out of the corner of my eye? How sweet this was going to be! Pete and I checked in at the table, stepped onto the Court, did a back stretch and bended far enough forward to touch our knees. Watch out Bills! The fun was about to begin.

As I ran down the court, all I wanted was for Pete to give me the ball. I should have been more attentive. Norwood set a pick. I wasn't paying attention. It felt like I had run into a brick wall. Two of my teammates peeled me off the floor. With gritted teeth and even greater determination to score, I told Pete to get me the ball. He did. A few dribbles and I was within two feet of the basket. I saw Reich positioning himself preparing to block any shot that I might attempt. "It can't get any better than this," I thought, "an out of breath forty-one year old man taking on a million dollar professional athlete, one on one." I only hoped the crowd appreciated what was about to happen.

I stopped on a dime, pivoted 180 degrees and with the greatest pump fake ever executed in the course of any basketball game, caused Reich to prematurely launch himself in mid-air, embarrassingly thwarting his plan to stuff the basketball down my throat. I laid the ball up and under his raised armpits. I saw the ball roll softly around the rim before it fell to the floor as all of that quarterback's six foot two inch frame crashed on top of me as I hit the court. What a move! The cheers of the crowd were deafening - Mike the small town attorney had just faked the pants off of a professional football player. All those Fridays of torture and pain had paid off. A whistle assured me of two foul shots.

As I positioned myself on the foul line, the referee handed me the ball. I bounced the ball repeatedly as I focused all my attention on the basket. I was still "pumped" and breathing heavily. I took a few deep breaths, calmed myself and let it rip. The first shot hit the front of the rim and bounced to the floor. "Got to make the next one," I told myself.

At the precise moment I released the second shot from my hands, the undetected, skillful and revengeful hands of quarterbacks Reich and Gelbaugh, who had stealthy positioned themselves directly behind me, grabbed the bottom of my shorts and in once precise flawless motion pulled them down to my ankles. The gasps and laughter of the players and the eight hundred fans in attendance verified that they had all seen more than they had ever anticipated seeing. Two things immediately came to mind: the proud shall be humbled and pick up your pants.

In a move just as smooth as the fake I had just executed, I pulled up my pants, ran down the court, and played defense.

The Man I Admire Most

Has it actually been twenty-eight years since I last looked into your twinkling blue Irish eyes or had the pleasure of being in your physical presence?

Some of the greatest and most influential individuals who have walked this earth have gone unnoticed save for those fortunate few who were blessed to walk in their steps. You are most definitely one of those special men.

You never acquired the power, property and prestige that so many in this world admire, value, seek and equate with success and greatness. You saw those items as "fool's gold" and chose to live a more simple but difficult life – a life of quiet dignity, hard work, good example, perseverance, loving concern, and faith in the Almighty. Although you were not given much material or educational advantages, you excelled in this life because you loved.

You had an insatiable and life long hunger for knowledge but willingly sacrificed your formal education in order to help your large family survive the ordeals of the Great Depression. You spent the rest of your life learning something new every day and relishing the acquisition of knowledge in so many fields. You knew more about so many different subjects than most college-educated individuals I have met. Oh, how you enjoyed listening to and engaging in the political debates over the pressing issues of your time!

You came from a large loving family so it is no surprise that when you married you welcomed seven new lives into this world. You were never a stranger to hard work. Your lack of formal education made it more difficult for you to get the better paying jobs. So you did what you had to do – you worked as many part times jobs as was necessary to supplement the income from your full-time position and to insure that your children would receive the quality formal education you had not.

Your work ethic did not go unrecognized and you were rewarded with a well-paying union position with a utility company. Yet, when you had to choose between doing what was right or going along with your

4

union bosses, you did what only men of integrity do – you did what was right.

You paid a steep price – loss of a well paying job and a return to a lifetime of multiple jobs in order to support your family. Some felt you were foolish for following your conscience and doing what was right. They were wrong. They should have admired your courage and conviction. Mom did. Your children do.

Despite the resulting struggles in your life, you never complained and we never felt deprived. We knew we were loved.

Somehow you made sure to find some time for each of us. How fondly, I remember the part-time penny arcade job you had in Times Square and how you would occasionally take one of us kids with you on Saturdays. You had the keys to all the games and we were able to play any and all of them for as long as we wanted and to have lunch with our Dad. How we were the envy of our little friends in the projects!

We were too young to remember the death of our two older brothers (one from polio and the other from pneumonia) or to appreciate the life-long pain and anguish you and Mom experienced from such a great loss. Even Mom's many and prolonged illnesses for more than 30 years was something you accepted - that's what love requires and what men of integrity do.

Even though you were a man of limited financial means, more than a handful of family members and friends told us at your wake how you had always shared what little you had to help those who had even less.

Though not formally educated, you were filled with a wisdom that comes not from books, a wisdom you freely shared when asked by those in need of direction and encouragement.

Few if any outside the family knew the personal burdens you carried. You loved people. You were a great listener. Everyone who got to know you respected you. You had a great Irish wit and charm about you. You were a skillful and well liked bartender and certainly enjoyed tipping a few with the boys at Cronin & Phelan when you were not tending bar. Your friends and clients there valued the compassion and wisdom that poured forth from your lips more than the liquid which flowed out of bottles and taps. They told me so as did the 25 foot banner they placed on the back wall behind the bar: "May Joe Seagriff rest in peace!"

Thank you for teaching me how to be a man — a man of integrity and of faith.

As I approach another birthday and my own eternal reckoning, know that my love and admiration for you is eternal.

When Life Throws You A Curve Ball

Carl was spending the afternoon watching football with his father and brother. This was in the day before satellite TV. The television reception was lousy. He was unable to rotate the roof antennae remotely. It was a bitter cold day where the winds bit into one's flesh like knives into steak. Everyone wanted to see the game, but no one wanted to go onto the roof and manually rotate the antennae. Carl, always anxious to please his father, bit the bullet, put on his coat, hat and gloves, went outside, climbed onto the roof, and freed the frozen antennae. He was looking forward to watching the game.

Three days later he regained consciousness in a hospital. He did not know it at the time but he was paralyzed from his shoulders down to his feet. He was totally immobilized, suspended face-down in mid-air, sandwiched between two metal frames with a "halo" crown screwed into his skull, much like the screws holding a Christmas tree trunk stable in its stand.

His life had been permanently altered in a way no one would consciously choose and most would angrily reject and curse. In the background, he heard voices and bits of a conversation he surmised was occurring between a doctor and his parents: "Given the extent of his injuries and paralysis, your son would be much better off dead."

In that instance, without a full appreciation of the extent of his injuries and the challenges he would face, Carl resolved to prove the doctor wrong. He determined then and there to live a full and satisfying life. And that, with God's grace, he did.

After months of extensive rehabilitation efforts, the only part of his body that Carl could move (or ever would be able to move for the rest of his life) was his head. That is all he had to work with - the only tool he was given with which to fashion the productive life he vowed for himself. It turned out it was more than enough.

He and his therapist worked tirelessly to strengthen those neck muscles – Hercules would have been envious of their success! This warrior spent hours with a straw-like stick in his mouth, learning to

7

communicate and to operate devices by using it to "peck away" at a computer keyboard. He then mastered the ability to operate a motorized and computerized wheelchair by blowing into a straw-like tube that had been positioned close to his mouth. He discovered that similar technology existed that would allow him to turn on lights, use and answer the telephone and open and close doors. It wasn't too long before Carl could sign an "X" to legal documents if you put a pen in his mouth. When his employer found out that Carl could operate a computer, he promised him a job. He also continued to keep Carl's insurance in effect.

It was now time, in Carl's mind, to leave the nursing home, to live at home and to go back to work. There was a slight hurdle he had to first overcome –it was cheaper for the insurance company to keep him in the nursing home than to pay for the specialized care and equipment he would need to live at home. What choice do you think that company made?

Nothing ever deterred Carl – not even insurance companies. It was a great day for this hero when his attorney walked out of the offices of one of largest health insurers with a settlement check and assurances to pay for the care and equipment Carl needed to maximize his desire to live a full and productive life. It was an equally great day, when he returned to work, and later when he married. He thoroughly enjoyed the annual pilgrimage to the Carrier Dome to watch his Orangemen take on the hated Hoyas while sipping down a few of those large "Dome" beers! Amazing what one can do with faith and determination.

Throughout our relationship, Carl never specifically mentioned God to me and sadly (at that time in my life), neither did I to him. But he had to know God – intimately so – in order to live as he did.

There were setbacks, frequent illnesses, too many hospitalizations and years later a divorce. But Carl never changed. He accepted whatever happened to him with stoic peace and resignation – even what many would consider the cruelest cross of all – untreatable cancer.

Even as he prepared for death, he did so with dignity and with the candor and frankness that characterized the way he interacted with those who were blessed to know him. Carl did not hesitate reminding us then (to our immediate shame but long-term benefit) to stop complaining about the minor trials and tribulations in our lives and instead to enjoy the life we have.

He taught all of us how to live and how to die.

Visit The Imprisoned

When we read or hear the Scriptural reminder of the eternal consequences for our failing to visit the imprisoned (Matthew 25: 31-46) more often than not the image that first comes to mind is of those locked behind bars in the far too numerous Federal and State prisons and local jails that saturate the landscape of this nation – some 2,266,800 adults in 2010 according to the U.S. Bureau of Justice Statistics. More than 2 million! Many of them are Catholic and none of them are there voluntarily!

Admittedly, Jesus is not calling every Catholic to be His representative and ambassador to our forgotten convicted brothers and sisters. Certainly though more are being invited to this needed ministry than are responding. Is God calling you? Is fear holding you back?

But there is one prisoner you need not fear - One that each and everyone who professes to be Catholic, without exception, is being called to visit. He has been imprisoned and been ignored for more than two thousand years. Unlike his 2,266,800 incarcerated brothers and sisters in the U.S., He is imprisoned voluntarily and out of love. Yet, the majority of those He loves and who profess to love Him ignore Him, rarely if ever visit Him.

He is in every Catholic Church where the Blessed Sacrament is reserved - but for all practical purposes, in too many instances – He is alone and abandoned. Even the few inclined to visit Him, often find the Church doors locked. How can that be for a Church and its members who are called to make the Eucharist, the source, center and summit of their lives? How can Love Himself be in our midst and so few care to be in His Presence?

Go visit your imprisoned Lord who longs to see you, listen to you, talk to you, and make you whole. He awaits you in the locked tabernacles of His Churches or exposed in a Sacred Monstrance.

During your visits, bless His ears and warm His Sacred Heart by repeating the loving words St. Maria Faustina offered Him:

"O Jesus, Divine Prisoner of Love, when I consider Your love and how You emptied Yourself for me, my senses deaden. You hide Your inconceivable majesty and lower Yourself to miserable me. O king of Glory, though You hide Your beauty, yet the eye of my soul rends the veil. I see the angelic choirs giving You honor without cease, and all the heavenly Powers praising You without cease, and without cease they are saying: Holy, Holy, Holy...I adore You, Lord and Creator, hidden in the Most Blessed Sacrament."

Visit this Prisoner as often as you can. Love requires nothing less.

You're Going To Miss "It"

It got to the point where I wanted to pull my hair out every time some well-intentioned family member or friend would tell me: "You're going to miss 'it'." Better do something before it is too late." I knew they all meant well. And they were right. I was going to miss "it". I had to and would address their concerns, but not just now. I kept assuring myself that I had plenty of time. The threatened loss of something I enjoyed so much was not imminent enough to convince me otherwise.

Months passed into years and years into a decade or two. I still hadn't got around to doing what I knew had to be done if I was to continue enjoying "it". My procrastination continued despite the never ending and persistent interior and exterior voices chirping over and over: "Come on. You have got to do it! You're going to miss "it" if you don't!"

They were still right. But I wasn't ready yet. I remained unconvinced that that day would ever come. I was enjoying "it" so much. I refused to heed their advice. In hindsight, this was quite foolish of me. After all, these were the folk who knew me best (foibles and all). They only wanted to help me continue to enjoy "it".

It was therefore very reassuring to see the faces of my family and friends as I awakened from a drug induced grogginess and fought my way back to consciousness. The great sense of relief evident on all their faces was soon replaced with a uniform shrill chorus of "We told you so! We told you so!"

Then just as quickly as the Red Sea parted, so did my family and friends, leaving just enough room between them to allow a person dressed in a crisp, starched, white linen coat approach me.

I saw the concern in his eyes. I could tell from the very first syllables that flowed from this man's lips that he was filled with compassion. It was obvious that he dreaded telling me that the day of reckoning and payback for my senseless and obstinate procrastination had arrived. I knew what he was going to say before his words entered my ears. As he leaned over to get close to me, family and friends did likewise. For

12

a split second the silence was so dense you could "have heard a pin drop". Then those words I never wanted to hear, I heard: "No more double bacon cheeseburgers for you!"

I am going to miss "it". I should have listened.

No One Picture Can Tell It All

The stately white columns of the reception hall's entrance stood out all the more because of the faded and weather beaten brick that surrounded it. The colorful rainbow of flowers that greeted its guests took their breath away. The slight summer breeze rustled everyone's hair as one by one family, friends and strangers passed through the massive iron doors.

Dad needed to rest. Even this short walk from the car presented a great challenge to lungs weakened by cancer. But he was determined not to let those destructive cells ruin this special day for his granddaughter. Amidst the internal agony unseen by those passing by, he stood tall and resolute, thankful to be there – a man who hours earlier nearly coughed himself to death. Amidst all these challenges, one could still detect that ever present but now fading twinkle in his blue Irish eyes.

As the bride and groom prepared to joyfully float into the reception area as only newlyweds can do, the comforting loved filled voice of a beloved granddaughter called out to my Dad: "This is for you Grandpa. We love you!" Seconds later the unmistakable sounds of an Irish bagpiper filled the room. Dad gluttonously and gleefully took in the precious sounds and relished the Gaelic green kilt worn by this skillful musician. O to be Irish and alive!

Dad was a humble, hard-working, loving man who sacrificed his education to help his Depression-era parents, a well-paying job instead of compromising his beliefs, and his own preferences in order to support a wife and seven children. He did so joyfully and without complaint.

Not one to have his picture taken, it took some cajoling from his granddaughter for Dad to pose for one on this most special occasion. How regal and majestic this simple man appeared, his hair (what was left of it) so meticulously combed, defiantly standing upright and proud in his white dinner jacket, unwilling to concede defeat to the cancerous army attacking him from within. I don't think Dad knew what a gift he was giving us that day.

It wasn't many weeks after this celebration that Dad's internal enemies got the best of him. He fought to the end, living long enough to hold another granddaughter's child, and his first great grandchild, in his then toothpick thin arms. As he gazed at God's newest creation, I am sure he was reliving the moments when he had held his own children, as well as the tortuous time he buried two of them.

Pictures are worth a thousand words, but no one photograph can tell the whole story.

Oh, to see again the twinkle in this Irishman's eyes! May he and all the souls of the faithfully departed rest in peace!

Campaign Surprises

Life is a series of phases. Each filled with various experiences and challenges. All require a response. Sometimes we fail; more often than not we succeed. But at every stage of our lives abundant surprises await us. Our responses to these unforeseen events are the threads we use to create either a life squandered or one well-lived.

Let me share a little bit about the "going public" part of my life. As someone who enjoyed laboring behind the scenes, one client at a time, I surprised myself when I decided to run for District Attorney. I had never been active in any political party. I had no money, no organization and no experience. Some said I had "no clue". But I did have a passion for "justice".

It is a difficult and humbling experience to run for public office. Collecting enough signatures to get your name on a primary ballot is a staggering task especially for someone inexperienced and without organized political support. Amazing how quickly friends and family can fill the gap.

I wasn't really surprised when the established politicians resented my challenging their incumbent (an honorable man) or when many of them refused to endorse or support me after I defeated him in a primary. I wasn't stunned to learn that a number in the party I now represented would actively work to defeat me. I wasn't shocked to learn that others were livid when I rejected their direction to participate in a "photo-op" with a visiting national political figure for whom I had little respect.

I can't say that I was stunned to learn that "the word went out" in a certain town that no one in the party was to lend me a helping hand or provide any public forum for me. I wasn't amazed when the media misquoted me, or when vile and false rumors circulated that my wife was planning to divorce me as soon as the campaign was over, or that there was an organized effort in certain areas to remove all of the campaign signs my supporters posted on my behalf. I can't even say that I was terribly astonished to have barely lost the general election, even though the majority of Republicans and Democrats voted for me.

There were many things, however, that did surprise me when I knocked on doors seeking sufficient signatures to have my name on the primary ballot. I will share just three.

"Good evening, sir," I said to a distraught-looking frail man who reluctantly opened the door of his home. I introduced myself and explained the purpose of my visit. With a venomous tone to his voice, he responded: "So Mr. big shot politician wants to see if my wife will vote for him? Ask her yourself." The harshness of his voice startled me as I hesitantly followed him into the living room. The second I saw his wife in bed, on oxygen and in the process of dying, I understood his pain and anger. "I am so sorry. I would not have bothered you or your wife had I known." "Get out," he shouted with tears in his eyes.

I left no longer keen about knocking on doors.

But no alternative existed. Night after night I would knock on the doors of strangers' homes, not knowing what to expect. One evening, a smiling grandmotherly lady (whom I had never seen before) opened her door and joyfully exclaimed, "Come on in. I've been expecting you. Have a seat young man. I'll get you some tea." Before I could say a word, she was off to the kitchen. She wanted to talk and show me each of the more than 100 clocks in her collection. When I would try to find a polite way of leaving, she would insist that I stay. There were more clocks to see. I kept looking at my watch but I stayed. I must admit she was a delightful and entertaining hostess.

After an eternity, I finally convinced her that it was time for me to leave. She understood and thanked me for giving her so much of my time. Then she told me she was sorry for having kept me there so long, admitting she had been a long time supporter of my opponent and had been requested by his supporters to detain me as long as she could should I stop at her home. As I left the company of this charming queen, she said with a twinkle in her eye, "I'm going to vote for you."

Perhaps the most surprising of the many experiences that occurred while I solicited signatures was how many times total strangers would sign my petition and then unabashedly and spontaneously ask if they could pray for me, not later but right then and there!

Losing is never pleasant but is often a blessing in disguise. Such was the case here. It was not important that I win but an essential thread in my life that I try.

It's Enough To Make God And A Grown Man Cry

What if you had given everything you had (including your life) in order that others might live but only a handful of those for whom you died seemed to care? What if you returned ready to comfort, strengthen and sustain them through life's daily challenges and struggles, but only a small number acknowledged your presence among them and even fewer spent time with you or sought your aid? What if the majority of people totally ignored you and acted as if you were not even there?

If you or I were treated this way, we would cry. Jesus, the King of King and Lords of Lords, is treated that way day after day by many who claim to be Catholic. Yet, so great is His love for us that He chooses to remain locked in the tabernacles of His churches, day after day, waiting for us to acknowledge His presence among us, to visit and speak to Him, and to ask for His help.

Today He too must have cried. I'll tell you why.

A man entered a Catholic church this afternoon to spend some quiet time in the soothing loving presence of His Lord. He was the only one there. He kneeled and prayerfully pleaded with Him to protect and heal his granddaughter and return peace to her young but troubled heart. The silence, solitude and flickering candles brought peace to his heart as this man gazed upon his imprisoned Lord.

This consoling silence was short-lived, however, as one parent after another arrived to pick up their elementary school age children from religious education class. It was not too long before this quiet and sacred place was filled with the din of loud adult voices discussing the burning issues of parenthood, politics and current economic challenges - no matter that their Lord was just a few feet in front of them; no matter the presence of a man obviously attempting to pray.

This man saw no visible evidence in the actions of these parents that any of them really believed that Jesus Christ was really and substantially present, Body, Blood, Soul and Divinity in the Sacred Eucharist reserved in the Church's tabernacle or that any of them even thought this would be an appropriate time for them to silently pray. As their children began to filter into the Church from the parish hall, bedlam followed them and the last vestiges of sacredness vanished, save for the one sole man sitting and silently praying, determined to offer good example. Maybe he should have spoken to these parents and their children. How will they learn if no one teaches or corrects them? No one did.

The conduct this man observed must not occur in the presence of such a loving God. It happened not only this afternoon but happens every Sunday in far too many Catholic parishes. These disrespectful behaviors will continue to occur so long as a majority of Catholics no longer believe that Christ is really and substantially present in the Eucharist.

Catholic Churches are intended to be sacred places – different from all other structures in which we spend time – a silent prayerful oasis of quiet, comfort, solace and grace. The stark reality that we have lost that sense and our belief in the Real Presence, is enough to make our Lord cry.

We must insist on reverent silence in our Churches. Hard to believe but we must re-teach this fundamental truth. Our every action while within our Church buildings must evidence our belief that we are in a sacred place and in the presence of God – otherwise the rest of what we teach or do in Church will be for naught.

It would be so easy to correct this tragic situation if our priests would remind us at Sunday Mass as to the proper way to conduct ourselves while in this sacred place and the reasons for doing so. Their instruction and example can be lovingly reinforced by conspicuously posting a reminder at all entrances that "Silence is the reverent language spoken here".

So why don't we? The continued failure to do so is what makes this grown man cry.

Of Hell and Other Things

After recently reading the familiar Gospel story about Lazarus and the rich man, I saw the following internet headline: "Pastor who does not believe in hell fired!" God's timing is impeccable, isn't it?

My immediate thought after reading this headline was "and this pastor was caught off guard by his dismissal?" The sad reality is that it is not just this specific minister, but so many other Christians, including many Catholics (even some of their priests), who have abandoned the fundamental truth that there are eternal consequences to a life lived in unrepentant and unconfessed sin (see Catechism of the Catholic Church, Sections 1033-1041).

"Our God is far too merciful," these dissidents argue, "than to banish anyone to an eternity in hell." What Scripture and what Catechism do they read?

How have we arrived at this state of confusion on such a crucial article of faith? When was the last time you heard a sermon on sin, death, hell, and the last judgment? Chances are not too recently. Been encouraged to go to confession regularly? How many funerals have you attended where the decedent's arrival in heaven has been happily and definitely announced? - far too many, probably.

The only way you can subscribe to a theory of universal salvation is to assume that God, His Church and the many individuals He has used over the centuries to teach and guide us never really meant what He or they said. You would have to conclude, for example, that the story of Lazarus and the poor man (Luke 16:19-31), the description of the Last Judgment (Matthew 26:31-46), and the Catechism references set forth above were never intended to be taken seriously. Maybe that is why verses 41-46 of Chapter 25 in Matthew are so often excluded when that Gospel is proclaimed in our Churches.

Of course, St. Augustine didn't really mean it when he said "God made you without yourself; God redeemed you without yourself; but God will not save you without yourself."

I am equally as certain that St. Bernard was faking it when with tears he said that "there was hardly one ship out of ten lost on the sea, but on the ocean of life there is hardly one soul saved out of ten."

What was Ven. Louis Granada, O.P. thinking when he opined that "Men have eyes as keen as those of an eagle in discerning the things of this world, but they are as blind as beetles to the things of eternity?"

Finally, I suspect that the late Father Winfrid Herbst, S.D.S. must have been hitting "the sauce" before he was foolish enough to write the following: "I am sure many lost souls in hell right now would cry out to preachers and writers if they could: Oh, why did you not tell us more about the horrors of hell? Why did you not strike such fear into our hearts by your realistic description of hell that we would have made greater efforts to avoid it?...Why did you spare our feelings in a matter of such eternal moment? Oh, why did you not make hell a thousand times hotter than you did, then perhaps we would not be here today? "

Where is the zeal for the salvation of souls?

God made us to be with Him eternally. He gives us all the graces we will need to join Him there. We can believe what He teaches, respond to His graces, humble ourselves by confessing and seeking forgiveness for our sins and enjoy eternity in His Presence, or we can reject what He teaches and offers us here on earth and discover to our eternal regret that God never lies. The choice seems so obvious, doesn't it?

St. Thomas Aquinas reminds us that no one "is in hell who did not have, time after time, the chance of taking heaven in his grasp". Father Leo Rudloff, O.S.B. reinforces the Angelic Doctor, when he stresses "that hell is not a blind destiny into which the sinner plunges unawares, but is his self-chosen and fully deserved portion."

We are entitled to the truth. Our priests and bishops must not hesitate to teach that truth, no matter how uncomfortable it may make them or us.

All I Want For Christmas...

As a six year old boy growing up in the 1950s there was nothing more I wanted for Christmas than my own *Lionel* train set. For weeks before Santa's arrival, I imagined the unending hours of joy I would have configuring various track layouts and designs, setting up train stations and track crossing gates, exercising full, unbridled and unimpeded control and authority over the transformer's throttle controls, deciding when the train was to chug down the tracks or when it would come to an abrupt stop. I would be the one to determine when to blow its whistle or when to release white pulsating puffs of smoke out of its jet black locomotive.

My older brother wanted trains as well. What if Santa brought me freight trains and Pete a passenger line? What if the jolly old guy also left lots of extra tracks? We could combine our sets and operate an expanded railroad line that would criss-cross the living room floor, go under the couches and chairs, out into the hallway, down into our bedrooms and back from whence they came. Maybe we could run the cat over along the way!

Mom and Dad were not too encouraging. They reminded us that there were lots of boys and girls that Santa would visit and not everyone could get everything they wanted.

I just knew Santa would not let us down.

As we got ready for bed that Christmas Eve, there was a knock on our 10th floor apartment door. We kids were startled. No one ever came to the projects for a visit at that time of night. We all wondered who was there.

"Go see who is knocking on the door, Pete," my Dad said. My brother was not only older than I but he was tall enough to see out the peep-hole. "It's Santa!" he screamed. "Let him in," my Father commanded. Pete did not hesitate for a second and opened the two door locks faster than I could have opened a can of soda!

It wasn't very long before my four siblings and I had a private audience upon Santa's lap. He was real! He knew our names, ages and where we went to school. He even reminded us of some of the naughty things we had done to each other. I still asked him for the trains!

I am not quite sure what kind of drink my Dad gave Santa, but he enjoyed it so much he asked for a few more.

After a short while a somewhat wobbly Santa got up off the couch and told us kids to go to bed and right to sleep if we wanted him to come back with our presents. We each gave him our final sales pitches, a hug goodbye and ran into our bedrooms. All of us, except my twin sister Jane, who fancied herself as the brightest of us kids. She had one remaining and unanswered question for Santa: "Since we don't have a chimney and fireplace and since you won't return if any of us are awake, who is going to unlock the door and let you back in?"

"Go to bed Jane," my Mom barked, sparing Santa from the need to answer such a pesky little question.

We all went to bed alright. But it took awhile before we fell dead to the world. It was actually only four and half hours later that Jane ran into our bedrooms screaming hysterically, "Get up! Santa's been here. You won't believe how much stuff he left!"

I knocked Jane over and flew down the hallway and into the living room. Mom and Dad were sitting together on the couch, waiting for their sizable brood to arrive. They looked exhausted but thrilled to see their children so excited.

I spotted the train sets immediately. Two of them! One freight and one passenger! Tons of tracks, trestles and accessories! I almost wet my pants!

The Power of a Promise Made and Kept

At a time of great personal and spiritual struggle in my life, my friend Jack invited me to a weekend retreat. He promised me that I would not regret going. He was right. That weekend God became very real to me and I began the life-long process of allowing Him to transform me.

In gratitude for His love, I promised God then I would share that love with others. Aside from my family, I was not quite clear where or how I would do this. Shortly thereafter, another "friend" invited me to come to prison with him. I was about to find out if I really believed that everyone (without exception) is made in the image of God and that with God all things are possible.

For more than ten years, I would spend Fridays through Sundays, three or four times a year in area prisons with total strangers. More often than not, when I arrived there, the bright sunlight would blindly ricochet off the sharp circles of razor wire affixed to the fences that surrounded the cold, depressing and unwelcoming structures in which these men were confined.

You really never get accustomed to visiting prison. Your every movement is monitored and orchestrated. There is a seemingly unending series of gates and/or doors to navigate. Always, without exception, one door or gate is opened and loudly closed behind you, before the locks securing the gate or door in front of you are slowly released. There is very little you can do there without first asking and obtaining permission. To easily distinguish visitors and staff from those serving time, all inmates were required to wear prison issued green pants. No one else wore green.

"Why," I often asked myself "did I continue to come back there?" "Because" I answered to no one in particular "I promised."

There are some people confined to these places who have repeatedly demonstrated a total disdain for lawful authority and the rights of others. More than a handful of them are supreme "con-artists" engrossed in only advancing their own interests. But each is someone's

26

grandfather, father, son, brother, uncle, nephew or grandson. Nearly all of them will be returned to our communities some day.

During the course of these weekends, we remind our "brothers in green" that God made each of them in His image, that He loves them and that they can have their lives transformed by Him. These are God's promises. This promised transformation will not happen overnight and will require a life-long commitment to follow Him each day. It can be lost just as easily as it was found. These are truths that some have either never heard before or had previously rejected. A few actually come to these weekends sincerely searching for a different way of life.

A sizable number initially come just to get away from the structured boredom of their daily routines and for the "real" donuts and coffee the volunteers bring from the outside. They have no real desire to change their way of life. They arrive with a great deal of cynicism and an unwillingness to be honest with anyone, including themselves. These captive souls often doubt the authenticity of their visitors and come to test them.

On one weekend we had a "Charlie Manson" look-alike at our table. They could have been twins. He meant business. He had intentionally come to the program with filthy clothes, smelling as if his body had never been touched by the cleansing and aromatic qualities of soap or deodorant. There was no way we would accept him, he thought. As difficult as it was, we did. Throughout the day, he challenged us and questioned us and then he began to listen.

When "Charlie" returned the next morning, he was clean shaven, freshly showered and wearing impeccably pressed green pants and white shirt. He was physically different. He joyfully interacted with us. He started the second day at least exteriorly different than he was the previous day.

He finished the day in the arms of a team member, crying uncontrollably and joyfully, having reconciled with his forgotten Lord through the Sacrament of Confession and having received Him in Holy Communion for the first time in twenty-seven years.

27

Then there was Juan. He was from Bolivia and spoke very little English. He was much younger than most of the other men attending this weekend. Unlike the vast majority of his peers, he was joyful and attentive from the outset. But he ate nothing during the course of the weekend – none of the exotic "goodies" we had brought and none of the prison meals that we all shared with each other. He just declined with a smile but offered no explanation. So when he joined us for Sunday dinner, we were all surprised.

After eating, he told us he had been praying for several months that God would send some people into the prison to encourage him in his spiritual walk. When he heard our group was coming, he decided to fast in thanksgiving to God for answering his prayer. He had not eaten any solid food since the previous Wednesday.

Who can forget Diego who broke down in tears when a team member hugged him at the sign of peace? With the exception of the physical contact he was subjected to by prison staff in performing their duties, this was the first time in over twenty years that a human being had demonstrated any physical sign of affirmation and affection to him.

What God can do with the promises we make and keep!

Not Forgotten

I have wondered occasionally what you must have thought when you first saw two little bodies squirming around in their cribs, squawking and demanding so much attention from others. Joseph, you were certainly old enough to understand who these two little runts were and why they required so much attention. But John, you were still in diapers and barely able to walk. You must have had some difficulty sizing up your new brother and sister and accepting your sudden relegation from king of the roost to third in line.

Jane and I certainly had no idea who you were or what kind of future we would all have together. I am sure my primary and sole focus at the time was to get fed and to be the center of attention. From family stories that I have heard, Jane had the same idea and the upper hand.

Knowing Mom and Dad, I doubt you guys ever felt neglected after our arrival. I suspect you both knew we were just two more creatures God sent for everyone to love. You were probably just as eager as everyone else that we grow up and be able to do fun things together. Our little sister Pat had more than enough love to "mother" us all. No doubt our brother Pete was prepared to lend a helping hand, whether he wanted to or not.

As one day rapidly turned into another, I am certain that Jane and I never tired of looking at you guys while we tried to figure out why you were on the other side of the crib and we were confined. On those occasions when we were momentarily set free, what havoc we probably wrought to your toys and special things. I am sure you couldn't wait until we were old enough where you could retaliate. I suspect John didn't wait.

But just as suddenly as we appeared in your lives, you disappeared from ours. Neither Jane nor I had any idea where you guys had gone or why joyful eyes were suddenly so red, swollen and sad. How quickly all our lives were changed. You never got to meet your little sister Flo.

Things like that happened back then before the arrival of penicillin or polio vaccine. How quickly pneumonia snatched the life out of John and polio briefly imprisoned Joseph in an iron lung before he too joined John with their heavenly Creator.

Every now and then I think of you guys and wonder what might have been. I need to do that more often. Thanks for letting us into your brief lives and for looking down all these years from above. Give Mom and Dad our love. Put a good word in for us.

With God's grace and counting on His mercy, I look forward to the time when our entire family will be united eternally in His Presence.

In the meanwhile, let's keep in touch.

For You!

For many weeks now, God has put it in my heart that I should write this. I kept putting it off - that has become my specialty since I retired! Not a good thing to do, especially after He was gracious enough to spare my life.

At a recent men's conference, He used a priest to remind me again to take a break from writing things for others to read and write to you. Even I will eventually catch on and do what He has asked! It is good that He is persistent but patient. There is much that I have to share, but today I will be brief (maybe not quite as you would like) and to the point.

Ready? I love you! I hope this is not startling news to any of you. But I may never have told you why. It is simple - because God loved you enough to create you in His image and then to give each of you to me to love, cherish, teach and return to Him. Just as we can reject Him, each of you could have easily rejected me. But none of you did. Each of you has chosen to love me – warts and all, good and bad – even at times when you may have had legitimate questions as to why you should. No words can ever adequately express the enormity of what the gift of your love means to me. You see - each of you have loved me in the very same way that God loves you.

Over the years, I have seen each of you grow in so many ways and have witnessed the immense size of your loving hearts. I have taken great pride in seeing how concerned each of you are not only about your immediate family but others whom you find to be in need of your time, your ears, advice, support, some tender love, compassion and concern. Each of you desires to make a difference in this world. Each of you has already done so in different ways and no doubt will continue to do so.

Life here on this earth is but a temporary journey during which we have many questions. The trials and struggles of our daily existence can sometimes weigh us down so heavily that we become despondent and wonder why our heavenly Father allows us to struggle so or permits such evil in this world. Just as you have on occasion not understood what or why I may have asked you to do or not do something, it is okay to have the same feeling about God.

Talk to Him! Ask Him for answers to the questions and concerns you find most troubling and upsetting. There are answers He will give you if you will humble yourself to ask them and if you are willing to put aside your opinion until after you have read authentic explanations of what He actually teaches and why, not what others mistakenly say He taught.

I certainly do not know everything (despite persistent vicious rumors to the contrary). No one does. I believe God allowed me to stay here among you so that I might finish the job He gave me and either accurately answer your questions on His behalf or refer you directly to someone or some resource that will honestly and reliably do so.

There is no other human being on earth that loves you more than I. At times I will disappoint you, but I will never ever mislead you about what God expects of us. I am not asking you to blindly accept everything that I tell you. But I pray that your love for me will cause you to give thoughtful consideration to, and not lightly dismiss, what advice I may be moved to share with you from time to time. I have been too afraid and cowardly to do that. Such fear and cowardice is offensive to God and deprives you of what a man must provide to those he loves. If I am to be at spiritual peace here and with Him at the end of this life, I must cast aside that fear.

Please never become upset with me when I share with you what is in my heart. I have no choice. God requires me to do so, even though there will be times when what I have to say may initially make you feel uncomfortable. I am not judging you. I am simply loving you by obeying Him and sharing His Truth. Ultimately, you remain free to accept or reject that advice, just as you are free to respond or reject the graces that God offers you each day. I will never love you any less than I do now. With God's grace I will love you more and more each day. But you honor Him and me when you love us enough to thoughtfully think about what we share – since all that we do or fail to do here have eternal consequences.

On the same token, you must continue to persistently (but lovingly) point out the many times that my actions are inconsistent with what I profess to believe or what I have tried to pass on to you as the Truth. Since Blessed John Paul II felt it necessary to go to confession every day, I suspect that you will have many, many opportunities to help me out in that regard. If we love each other in this way, God will lead each of us to Him, we will find satisfaction in our earthly lives, and we will be together eternally - and isn't that what this life is really all about?

Please do me one more favor. Every now and then, ponder the following truths and live your lives accordingly: "God made me. God loves me. God wishes to spend eternity with me!"

When I saw most of you around my hospital bed nearly five years ago and when later I read what you wrote about me, I knew what a very blessed man I was to have each of you in my life.

Let me love you as I ought and for however long I will be here with you. But keep me honest.

No, Not That Picture!

It was nice to have the family and in-laws all together for dinner. With my siblings and their children living such long distances away, it wasn't easy to get everyone in one place at one time. Everyone had arrived. It was going to be a special day!

About an hour later, my daughter started passing around pictures of her children. This encouraged others to share photos they had in their purses or wallets. We were all having a good time.

Suddenly, my son yells over to me. "Hey Pops, why don't you show the 'fam' what you looked like way back when you were in college?" With a mischievous look on his face and a twinkle in his eye, he shouted, "I'm sure your nieces, nephews and grandchildren would love to see what 'Mr. Conservative man' looked like back then!" "There's nothing interesting to see," I replied. "Anyway, I wouldn't be able to find any pictures now. Let's watch the football game."

From the corner of my eye, I saw my wife rumbling through a box in the hallway closet. I asked her what she was looking for. "Don't worry," she replied. "I found it." With a smile on her face and tears rolling down her cheeks she announced to the assembled family, "Wait 'til you see it! You're going to love it." Before I could get that picture out of her hands, she ran across the room to an ever expanding circle of family eager to see what she had retrieved.

"What are you showing them?" I growled at the snickering group of laughing hyenas standing around the living room. "Stop laughing," I pleaded. "It's not that funny." "O yes it is," my lovely bride exclaimed. "This is priceless," echoed her sister. "Just look at the expression on Mom's face." Even though she was in this photograph and hated having her picture taken, my mother-in-law Ada was all for everyone having a look. In fact, she was laughing and crying so hard, I feared she would flood the living room floor.

"Okay," I said, "you've had your fun. Enough is enough." I lunged at the photo but it landed in my son's hands. "Pops," he shouted, "this isn't that bad. Do you mind if I put in on Facebook and share it with your colleagues and friends?"

"That," I assured my hysterical son, "would be your last living act." He walked towards me and with gleeful eyes handed me the picture. "Don't worry Pops, your former life will not see the light of day."

I glanced at the picture. I too laughed until tears were rolling down my face. "How could I have allowed myself to look like that?" I exclaimed. A picture, they say, is worth a thousand words. This one was encyclopedic!

Remember this tale the next time someone asks you if they can take your picture.

Christmases Past

Most of us recall the joy and excitement we experienced as young children singing Christmas carols and happy birthday to Jesus while waiting to see what gifts Santa would leave under our tree. How many times did my siblings and I resolve to catch the jolly old man in the act only to fall fast asleep – many hours later then Mom and Dad would have liked? Strange how we could not quite understand why they looked so tired as we exploded into their bedroom at 3 A.M. and at fifteen minute intervals thereafter until they finally conceded defeat, crawled out of bed, and witnessed our glee and excitement.

After becoming parents ourselves, we acquired a greater appreciation for the many sacrifices Mom and Dad had made to bring joy to our silly trusting little hearts. Of course, Christmas was not Christmas unless we went to Church, left a gift, and had a special dinner. Those of us blessed with such precious memories have done our best to re-create them for our own children and grandchildren. I treasure all those memories. There have been, however, several unique Christmases that helped me better understand the reason for celebrating Christ's birth. Three of them stand out in my mind.

In 1968 I was more than 8000 miles from home, in a nation at war. We spent much of a brutally hot and humid day, filling sandbags to reinforce our sagging bunkers, only to spend most of that night in those same shelters, seeking to shield ourselves from a seemingly unending barrage of rocket and mortar fire. The night was not silent. There was no peace; little good will was evident. This is what happens when men forget the Prince of Peace.

Fifteen years later, some 20 miles from home, I found myself surrounded by an ocean of razor wire and unwelcoming prison staff, upset they had to be on duty instead of being with their families. The inmates we came to visit, on the other hand, radiated the joy and peace of the Season, appreciative that someone cared enough to come as a representative of a merciful and forgiving God. Tears of gratitude for this gesture of love flowed from Juan's eyes, as he handed me a Christmas card. It had cost him $2.50, his entire weekly salary. It was my turn to cry.

In 2007, our son came home for Christmas. How excited my wife and I were to pick him up at the Rochester airport Christmas Eve, his cross country flight so long delayed because of wintry weather conditions. What a great Christmas gift was Joe! We enjoyed his company as we chatted nonstop during the drive home, arriving there at 1 A.M.

He was exhausted. It was difficult to just drop Joe off there and immediately leave but we had a long anticipated commitment to fulfill. Our son understood that a magnificent gift awaited his parents just a mile away. It was quiet and peaceful as we entered the Adoration Chapel in our Church where for the next two hours we were blessed to celebrate Christmas with and to be in the presence of the Prince of Peace.

Crosses or Toothpicks?

Let me repeat some obvious truths. God is more powerful than any of us. He draws each of us to Himself. He wants to excite our hearts. He longs to fill our minds and souls with the Truth. He desires that we yield ourselves totally to His will. We are often reluctant to do so because we know we may be mocked, laughed at and persecuted. In truth, our fidelity to God and His Word may bring us pain and suffering. It is so difficult to follow Him. At times we don't want to do as He asks. What He wants from us sometimes seems too painful, too difficult, and too burdensome. We want to flee and hide from Him. But we can't. He is everywhere. He has given us Himself. Our salvation and that of others hinges on our sharing and living this Truth. So we must go on - imperfectly and inconstantly no doubt - but we must go on, trusting that God will be at our side.

One of the reasons we don't always trust Him is our failure to understand the necessity and value of the suffering He asks of us. In our current world, many of us do everything we can to avoid suffering. We see little meaning in it. Like Peter's initial reaction, we often scold or mock those who talk of it or seek it. We look at suffering as men do, not as God does. What reluctant and unwilling cross bearers many of us have been! But Jesus lets us know in the Gospel of Matthew (16:24) that we can not be His followers if we do not take up our crosses and follow Him.

So what are we reluctant cross bearers to do? Perhaps these words of St. Francis de Sales will help:

"The Everlasting God has in His wisdom foreseen from eternity the cross that He now presents to you as a gift from His innermost heart. This cross He now sends you is considered with His all-knowing eyes, understood with His divine mind, tested with His wise justice, warmed with loving arms and weighed with His own hands, to see that it be not one inch too large and not one ounce too heavy for you. He has blessed it with His Holy Name, anointed it with His grace, perfumed it with His consolation, taken one last look at you and your courage, and then sent it to you from heaven, a special greeting from God to you, an alms of the all-merciful love of God. "

By taking these words to heart, we might recognize some of the crosses we most dread to carry are no more than toothpicks and that, by God's grace, no cross He sends will ever be too heavy.

Is This The End?

Neither my wife nor I had ever driven across country. We were excited to do so since the prize awaiting us in Denver was an extended visit with our daughter Tammy and her husband. We planned a leisurely trip with no set schedule, driving as far or as little as we cared to do on any particular day. We gave no thought to weather conditions along our planned route, assuming the high blue sky and feather like clouds that had been with us from the outset of our journey would accompany us throughout our trip.

We drove past blighted inner cities, congested and traffic logged interchanges in and about Chicago, and the unending miles of corn fields and irrigated farmland that would stretch before and around us as we traveled through Iowa and Nebraska. I must admit that I enjoyed driving at 85 miles an hour, amused and perplexed however that everyone was passing me.

We spent two relaxing days in Des Moines, Iowa to break up the trip and give my ailing back a break. Refreshed, we headed west anxious to see and experience the steep and majestic Rocky Mountains in Colorado. We almost didn't make it.

Somewhere between Des Moines and Omaha, Nebraska, realizing I had forgotten to fill up the tank, I took the first exit that displayed a gas station sign. Little did I know then that in many parts of Nebraska, gas stations are miles and miles off the exit – in this case 26 miles to be exact. Fortunately we made it, filled up, drove back to the four lane interstate racetrack we had previously exited and resumed our journey. There was a steady flow of traffic in our two westbound lanes, both behind and in front of us. It wasn't long before I was back at 85 mph and marveling again at all those who flew past us.

Just minutes later, without any warning, the blue sky was swallowed up by instant darkness. Vicious streams of rain poured down upon us, accompanied by vile and strong winds.

Even with the windshield wipers working at full speed, I had great difficulty seeing more than a few feet in front of me. I was going too fast at the time to safely pull off on the shoulder. I began to slow down so that I would be able to do so. Within seconds we were surrounded by an impenetrable brown cloud and a wind that began pushing our vehicle as it pleased. I could see nothing. I did not know what lane I was in, or whether the road ahead of me was straight or curved. I had no idea how close I might be to any vehicle in front of me, or how anyone approaching us from the rear would ever be able to avoid hitting us.

The fear in my eyes only added to the terror evidenced on my wife's face. I told Lonnie I loved her; she expressed her love for me. We both prayed that God would be merciful to us, as I slowly inched the car toward what I hoped would be the shoulder of the road. I had no way of knowing where I was.

The minute I silently accepted our impending deaths, I received an unmistakable, non-verbal, internal prompting to stop the car. It made no sense! But I did as I was prompted.

The wind picked up, our car began to rock from side to side. We were sure the force of the wind would flip us upside down. An eerie indescribable noise surrounded our vehicle. A vise grip could not have held Lonnie and me any closer than we were. Her finger nails dug deeply into my arm and shoulders. Tears were flowing from her frightened eyes; my heart almost jumped out of my chest.

As quickly as this nightmare began, it ended. The wind was no more. The brown fog lifted. Where once there was the sound of impending death, now there was a deafening silence of absolute stillness. We were alive! We gave thanks to God and kissed each other like it was our very first time.

I looked out the window, now able to clearly see all around me. I couldn't believe my eyes. For reasons known only to Him, God had safely placed our vehicle on the shoulder of an exit ramp, just feet from a nearly empty parking area!

Where Have They Taken Him?

When I travel and enter unfamiliar Catholic Churches, I don't really ask for much: an atmosphere of reverent silence and a tabernacle in front of which I may momentarily kneel and worship my Eucharistic Lord.

One would expect our Lord to be in "a distinguished place... conspicuous, suitably adorned and conducive to prayer". But often His whereabouts are unknown. Far too often, instead of kneeling before the King of Kings and Lord of Lords, I have to assemble a search team to scour the Church building to find out where they have taken Him! This should never be! But it occurs far too frequently.

My daughter and her family recently moved to a new town in a new State. We went to visit them. We also went to visit our Lord in the two Catholic Churches located in this town. He was no where to be seen! After searching for Him in the larger of the two Churches, I found Him in a chapel set apart from the area where the congregation gathers and celebrates Mass. I never did find where they had taken Him in the other Church!

A few days before this upsetting experience, I was blessed to attend the annual conference of the Catholic Marketing Network and the Catholic Writers' Guild. These groups had no difficulty placing a tabernacle prominently behind the altar that had been set up in one of the hotel's banquet rooms.

They also had no problem processing with our Eucharistic Lord from the hallways of one hotel to repose the Sacred Monstrance in an Adoration Chapel set up in an adjoining hotel. This all took place in a secular setting with hundreds of committed Catholics unabashedly and publicly singing "Holy God, We Praise Thy Name".

Our Church buildings must be sacred places in which the tabernacle where Our Lord resides is prominently and conspicuously placed and readily visible to everyone upon entry. No one should ever have to search for Him after entering His Church.

How blessed I was to give witness to my belief in His Eucharistic Presence by processing with Him through the halls of two secular buildings. How tragic that I could not readily find Him in two of His Churches.

He Visited – How About You?

From the inception of the Adoration Chapel in our parish and without interruption for nearly five years until a few days before his death, this gentleman came every Saturday morning. Initially, he came for two hours each week – from 3 A.M. to 5 A.M. Eventually, another person lent a helping hand by coming in a half-hour early each Saturday morning. That hour and a half was not enough for Mike – he added another hour each week when he joined his wife in the Chapel each Monday evening.

He learned to pray the Rosary there. Oh, how he enjoyed praying the Rosary before the Blessed Sacrament!

Nothing kept him away – not snow, not ice, not radiation treatment, not chemotherapy, not even a terminal illness. Just weeks before his death, he came in at 3 A.M. in obvious discomfort. He was coughing and had some difficulty breathing. But how devoutly he tried to genuflect and bow his head before his beloved Lord. After awhile, he settled in his chair, pulled out his favorite little meditation booklet and began to pray the Rosary.

He knew that others were willing to cover his hour and half for him. But he did not want to "inconvenience anyone". Despite the cancer that was raging through his weakened body "there was no reason for him to give up his hour yet," he said, "except that he was getting a little lazy." His fellow Adorers reminded him of all the prayers being offered for him during this difficult time and of their desire to be helpful to him and to his family. He appreciated everyone's prayers and concerns and simply told us that he did not want to get angry with God. He never did.

"It was okay for you to leave," he said to the person he was relieving. "No need to stay. I'll be fine." Mike was at peace – one with his heavenly Father and Mother. We should have all thanked him then for teaching us how to live and how to die – with absolute trust and faith in a God Who always knew what was best for him.

My friend spent his last hour before the Blessed Sacrament with his wife five days before he passed away. He died at home surrounded by his loving family and on the feast day of Our Lady of the Rosary. How great is our God!

This simple and humble man would have been the first one to admit that there was nothing of any value that he ever did on his own. Anything of value that he did (and he did much of eternal value) was only by and through the grace of God. How abundantly willing He is to provide that grace to those who love Him!

God does not promise those who love him a life here free of trials and tribulations. Time before Him in the Blessed Sacrament is no guaranty of a struggle free life. But He does promise sufficient graces to carry our daily crosses **and** eternity with Him for those who love Him.

Mike loved to visit Him. You will too! Our Lord is waiting for you! Please do not disappoint Him - so many who claim to be His followers have and continue to do so.

I Will Give You a New Heart

I walked out of the State Capitol building and immediately turned to my left looking beyond the many different people walking about the area and in the nearby park until I saw her. There was my smiling wife, just a few feet from me, eagerly awaiting news of what transpired during my interview. I approached her excitedly wanting to fill her with the details as soon as I could. But suddenly I did not feel well. A strange sensation overtook me - a very uncomfortable, unfamiliar and unsettling one.

She immediately saw that I did not look "right". There was no time to discuss the interview. I told her that we should try to get some aspirin before we picked our car up in the underground garage. She was, of course, very concerned.

It was difficult walking down the street, across the roadway and up the stairs and into the building where I had worked several years previously. Fortunately, there was still a little store on the second floor just as I had remembered. I asked Lonnie to go there and see if they had any aspirin.

As she left to go, I sat down. I began to sweat profusely. I had no pain; but I was not right. One of the security officers saw me and summoned a retired emergency medical technician who was on duty. He immediately called for assistance, removed my suit jacket, tie and dress shirt.

By then my wife had returned. I saw her standing in the background but it was so surreal. My struggling and stressed heart almost broke as my chest tightened and I saw the anguish, fear and tears flowing from her eyes. Oh, I wanted so much in some way to spare her from this experience. I was powerless to do anything other then to sit down in the rapidly expanding pool of sweat that enveloped me. What would be, would be. "God," I prayed, "be merciful to me a sinner. Be with and comfort my wife."

The medics arrived quickly. They calmly and reassuringly went about their task of trying to save my life. I was in route to Albany Medical

Center, when I was suddenly "prompted" to ask them to take me to St. Peter's Hospital instead.

We arrived at that hospital a few minutes later. They wheeled me rapidly through a crowded emergency room and into an examination stall. Instantly, a nurse and doctor appeared. Just as quickly, they whisked me out and up to the operating room. A whirlwind of activity occurred as I lay on a cold metal table with nurses and doctors speaking to me. I held my precious rosary beads in my hand and continued praying to my Lord. "An excellent thing to do," I heard one of the hospital staff say.

"Mr. Seagriff," a doctor said, "one of your arteries is completely blocked; one is sixty percent blocked and a third forty percent blocked. You are having a heart attack and we are going to try to unblock them and insert stents."

Surprisingly, I did not panic – something that would have been my normal *modus operandi* under such dire circumstances. In an inaudible spiritual voice, I calmly told my God that I did not want to die but if that was His will for me then so be it. I told Him how sorry I was for my sins and for squandering a good portion of my life, asked Him to have mercy on me, to forgive me, and to strengthen and protect my family. I resumed moving my fingers along the Rosary beads as God directed the hands of my doctor and his staff.

Nearly five years have elapsed since God spared my life. Only He knows why I am still here. While pondering that very thought recently, I discovered a journal entry that I had made the day **before** my heart attack. Over the years I have not been very faithful or successful in journaling on any regular basis. So it was not surprising that I had not only forgotten I had made any entry that day, but it was purely fortuitous I even found it since it was on separate sheet of paper, stuck in a file folder that had nothing to do with my journal.

I read the entry. My face became flush. My heart raced and tears flowed. You see the entry that day – the day before my heart attack - reflected my thoughts on a promise God made to the prophet Ezekiel:

"The world will know that I AM the Lord, and that I am holy by the example you give...Not on your own but by means of my transforming grace, I will cleanse you of your impurities and make a new creation of you. I will give you a new heart and a new spirit I will put within you. I will remove the heart of stone and give you a natural heart. I will put my spirit within you and make you live by my statutes, careful to observe my decrees." (Ezekiel 36:23, 25-27)

This is what I wrote that day:

"How Christ-like am I? Have I surrendered myself to His transforming graces? Do I draw others to Him? - not on any regular basis. Lord that I may surrender my entire being to you and allow You to use me as You will.

Astonishing isn't it! God offers us eternal happiness with Him in heaven. Yet most of us do not want it. We prefer to do things our own way. How many times has God invited me into His service and how many times have I refused to come?"

The day after this entry, God opened three arteries, giving me the new heart and new spirit He promised the prophet and for which I prayed the day before my heart attack.

Every day I must honestly ask myself: What have I done with this new heart? God knows. Does anyone else?

About the Author

Michael Seagriff practiced law for 30 years, as a general practitioner, prosecutor, criminal defense attorney and Administrative Law Judge.

His vocation as a Lay Dominican created an insatiable desire to learn, study, live and share his Faith. For more than ten years he led a Prison Ministry program and has spent the last decade promoting Perpetual Eucharistic Adoration, serving as coordinator of that devotion in his former parish. He always wanted to write and share these experiences but never seemed to have the time when he was working. All that changed unexpectedly in 2009 when he retired.

Articles that he has written since retiring have been published in *Homiletic & Pastoral Review*, *The Catholic Sun*, a weekly diocesan newspaper, *Catholic Exchange.com*, *CatholicLane.com*, *Catholic Online*, *Catholic Writers' Guild Blog*, and *Zenit*.org.

The author acquired his healthy sense of humor and his love for the Catholic Faith from his deceased Dad and employs both frequently, sometimes to the joy and at other times to the consternation of those closest to him.

He blogs at: http://harvestingthefruitsofcontemplation.blogspot.com/.

Other Books By Author

Forgotten Truths to Set Faith – Words To Challenge, Inspire and Instruct is the recipient of the Seal of Approval from the Catholic Writers' Guild.

This book is a compilation of over 1200 essential but *Forgotten Truths* that opened the author's eyes, spoke to his heart and stirred his soul. The power of these words changed his life and can do the same for all who read and reflect upon them.

****

Pondering Tidbits of Truth - If we spend little or no time pondering the truths and mysteries of our Faith, we are not going to progress spiritually - a growth essential to our eternal well-being and that of those around us.

Pondering Tidbits of Truth gives you a tool to do both. This book recognizes two realities of contemporary life: we are all busy people and many of us have convinced ourselves that we simply do not have the time to read, ponder and reflect on the wealth of spiritual wisdom our Catholic Church has accumulated over the centuries. Yet, we owe God and ourselves this reflective time.

Among the 100 quotations in this book, some may be familiar to you - others maybe not so much. All of them offer much fruit for your reflection and contemplation.

Soft and Kindle versions of both these books can be purchased on Amazon.com.